FLIGHT PLAN

FLIGHT PLAN

poems

☽

M. Soledad Caballero

Red Hen | *Pasadena, CA*

Book design by Em Villaverde.

Library of Congress Cataloging-in-Publication Data

Names: Caballero, M. Soledad, 1973– author.
Title: Flight plan: poems / M. Soledad Caballero.
Description: First edition. | Pasadena, CA: Red Hen Press, 2025.
Identifiers: LCCN 2025012188 (print) | LCCN 2025012189 (ebook) | ISBN
  9781636282527 (paperback) | ISBN 9781636284361 (library binding) | ISBN
  9781636282534 (ebook)
Subjects: LCGFT: Poetry.
Classification: LCC PS3603.A26 F55 2025 (print) | LCC PS3603.A26 (ebook)
  | DDC 813/.6—dc23/eng/20250414
LC record available at https://lccn.loc.gov/2025012188
LC ebook record available at https://lccn.loc.gov/2025012189

The National Endowment for the Arts, the Los Angeles County Arts Commission, the Ahmanson Foundation, the Dwight Stuart Youth Fund, the Max Factor Family Foundation, the Pasadena Tournament of Roses Foundation, the Pasadena Arts & Culture Commission and the City of Pasadena Cultural Affairs Division, the City of Los Angeles Department of Cultural Affairs, the Audrey & Sydney Irmas Charitable Foundation, the Meta & George Rosenberg Foundation, the Albert and Elaine Borchard Foundation, the Adams Family Foundation, Amazon Literary Partnership, the Sam Francis Foundation, and the Mara W. Breech Foundation partially support Red Hen Press.

First Edition
Published by Red Hen Press
www.redhen.org

ACKNOWLEDGMENTS

The author would like to thank the editors of the following publications in which some of these poems first appeared.

Coalhill Review: "Gravity, or After the Plane Crashes"; *Cutthroat: A Journal of the Arts*: "Myths We Tell"; *The Familiar Wild: On Dogs & Poetry*: "Of Names and Numbers"; *Iron Horse Literary Review*: "Dear Poem," "Ghosts Don't Live by Our Rules"; *Lunch Ticket*: "All Love Stories are Death Stories," "Follow-Up," "Stage Two"; *The Missouri Review*: "1978," "Oddfellows 215"; *Nimrod International Journal*: "The Mirage"; *Orange Blossom Review, a Journal of Creative Arts*: "Writing Poetry after Turning 46"; *Poetry Northwest*: "Ode to Kody"; *Queen Mob's Teahouse*: "BoneBreakers"; *Slippery Elm*: "Flying, a list," "When We Won Blue Jays at the Aviary"; *SWWIM Every Day*: "Before an MRI, a Questionnaire"; *Tinderbox Poetry Journal*: "I Continue My Love Affair"; *Twyckenham Notes, Contemporary Art & Poetry*: "Adjustment Disorder, Part I or Weekly Therapy After Cancer," "El Rio Bravo del Norte"; and *Vida Review*: "The Myths We Live," "On the Phone with My Mother after She Watches the News."

for Richard

Contents

FLIGHT PLAN

Let Emptiness Be the Prize

I am now of an age when I occasionally think
my body is not able to have children anymore;

not that I have ever thought about or wanted
them, so I am grateful for this sagging, browning

empty body that cannot craft a zygote into a fetus
into a human with my DNA and fear of horses; it's true

I am occasionally sad about the decades I've lived
too quickly, how my skin bunches around my stomach

from the years of cheese and wine, I mean it's not a brilliant
thing to be a woman of a certain age, I don't care what

Virginia said about a room and some cash to write.
Clarissa Dalloway had three lovers at least, and at the end

of her party she feared the war dripping off the young
man's body, or at least that he reminded her that she too

would end up falling to a quiet death. Still, even with that
husk of a prospect, I am grateful this sack of mine is made

of dried fruit, apricots, cranberries, other sugared sweets,
and yes, I am in awe of my small acorn ovaries shriveled

from chemo and other toxins with no lingering warmth
for any green to grow; but to be a woman with burnt ovaries,

to flaunt the ecstasy I can still plunder from between
my legs, that is a joy not allowed. Because what woman

gets a chance to celebrate her body's lack of birthing, to cheer
for blood that never gets to be more than blood?

I will celebrate this body, ragged, jagged, far too big and wild
for every day, and I will let its emptiness be the prize.

ON THE PHONE WITH MY MOTHER AFTER SHE WATCHES THE NEWS

On the phone she talks to me and her voice is liquid, like the ocean after a storm when the sun and the rain are the same over the horizon. She tells me, I say nothing. I keep my mouth shut. Me hago la loca y la ciega, she whispers. Me hago chiquitita como un grano de arroz. When she tells me about her mother, mi vieja linda, que linda era mi vieja. When she tells me about the summers she spent in the granja, how there were grapes and goats and the cheese was fresh like dough before it rises. She remembers those moments as if they are dancing to her words. When she tells me about her silence and the way she keeps quiet, keeps small, I think about the way her voice sounded on the cassette tapes she recorded for her mother her sisters her brother decades ago when the phone was too pricey for her voice. She whispered about the snow and the gray goblin oil machines, the way the grass moaned across the prairie for hours even in the middle of summer. Her voice was a song, even when she learned English, heard it break out of her mouth like thin glass and she could not say sheet without shit and now that feels exactly right, the way things are is shit if she has to keep her song stuck behind her tongue, stuck to the back of her throat like a rag. No digo nada, no digo nada, me hago muy muy chiquitita she says when they ask her about home and the Andes and about the accent that still lingers, rattles in her throat in her teeth. This is home, she says, this is home this is home, les digo eso she says to me now when I ask her how the desert smells, how the saguaros look when the flowers bloom in spring. No, she says, I say nothing, me río hehehehe, me hago la lesa. Así no me molestan, así me dejan sola, mijita. She says this is the way to be safe to be whole to be ignored to be out of the way.

ALL I HAVE ARE ELEGIES

There is no before for this body. No what was.
Just a blank sheet of frozen water covering
the whole world. I have read cells replicate trauma
from years when we were not even part of the stars.
I do not know about skin memory, what organs
remember, what my body knows still about
dying cells, deadly small beasts growing inside.
My body is charred bits writhing, hidden in
the microscopic parts of my bones, my mouth.
What I know is I am this body now, an oozing
egg yolk that must imagine itself whole.

BONEBREAKERS

The bones will rise, that is what Ezekiel says.
Gray and dusty, buried beneath the dirt, the sand,
the rocks and dry leaves. They have been there
for decades, have been like chalk, like old flour,
so thin, so empty of breath. These are the bones
to be lifted. They will have breath blown into them,
like a whirlwind of life. Skin will grow, thick muscle,
tendons, blood. Ezekiel says that all the parts will grow
like moss, like algae on the water. Spreading everywhere,
covering the skeletons of the dead with layers of
tissue and organs. In the story, this is the sign of God,
promises made in the book of time when there were
old men who waited for signs in the sky and in the trees.
God signs, even after so many years as dirt.

Families climb, crawl, drag bones that already
have breath. Hearts that already beat.
They have breath. They are not silent with death.
They wish for lands of light. Families reach the borders,
a prophecy of hope. Children come to this land
of stone and grit and blood holding their fathers' hand,
holding onto their sisters' hand, holding on, still
breathing, still alive in the midday sun.

We take them, make meat of the hearts,
the bones, the children. We mark them
with words of salt. We cage them in
frozen cement. We use bricks. We use fists.
We use teeth. We use bare hands.
We are harbingers of dust and wounds.
We break bones. We are bone breakers.

Adjustment Disorder, Part I
or Weekly Therapy after Cancer

At first, I think: she is a child.
She is playing the part of seer.
What can she know about mutating
things swimming in a body. What can she
know of that midnight blue moment
of breathless fear, when you wake up,
feel the cells of your heart are
rebelling, making an army right inside
the ribcage, penetrating the liver,
weaving up through the bloodstream
into your breast again. A snake,
thick, gray mamba so beautiful, so deadly.
She tells you yes, yes this is normal.
Yes, this is fear. It will feed you ash
until you look at it. You try to look
at it. The angular curved scale of it,
this gaunt thick gut creature that chases
you through morning rituals, coffee,
breakfast, brushing your teeth before work
when you look in the mirror and think, *it is back.*
It has found fresh ground to harvest.
The mole there, that stain of skin,
that looks strange. Faded patch
of skin under your arm, has it grown?
The woman you talk to tells you
this is part of the story. It will pass.
You want to thank her. But this snake lives
in the membrane, the thick brown gristle
of your memories. She cannot know
its bulbous mouth, strange succubus
standing just to the left of your life.

GRAVITY, OR AFTER THE PLANE CRASHES

What is gravity
                    in the middle

          of a black
                              ocean?
Again
          this year

          bodies
                    fell
                              through the sky,

                              bodies
fell through

          the blue
                              holding hands.
They landed naked

          in the water
          still
          holding

                              hands.
Families fainted.

They watched screens.
                              Hands

                              bodies

their beloved

      floating

      in cold

              dark water.

In waves
and wind
and violent

              under pull.

Where do the living   the dead things

              meet

when skin and love

      go missing in   the middle

of purple water   when gravity exists

              only

to offer

      limits.

      We still

              hold
              hands,

      Watch

while the mystery

              of life goes

under and the bodies

sink

and the families

hold hands

wait for tokens

try to forget

the blind
slimy creatures
that live

on the gravity

that still

works   in

death.

MYTHS WE TELL

Act I.

On the plane, I cried, little understanding my mother's tears, her sorrow,
the years she would live inside herself, her heart eaten by time, battle

weary from the harsh, grasping noise of prairie ghosts and English.
I think of her now as I walk across airports, watching other mothers,

the way they cradle a daughter on hips, whisper to a boy running down
the hallway to be careful with his body. They are more than gods.

Their bodies soft, meaty, aching from years of love and silence. Wanderers
lost in the middle of the story, in the middle of a wish, like the sun just

as it plunges into water, strange and silent. My mother was like them.
For thirty-five years she held our lives in her body, in her hands, in the back

of her throat, a mermaid with green eyes and a green voice trying to escape
from the daily planet of my father's rage, his dank disappointments.

My mother lived in cracked English, every day whispering gray prayers.
Every day she wished for the land of snow and love to free her.

Act II.

Every day, my mother wished for the land of snow and love to free her.
She landed in Oklahoma and was a lost queen in a gray castle, stuck

inside cement and time, waiting for her life to become hers, wishing
for water and sand and sun to carry her across into the warmth of any

miracle, or to give her enough love to make more of the brittleness
of daily things. She trudged across those years with no English in her

mouth, begging to the gods. She walked across the hard, teeming snow,
thin and sleep deprived. She lived in a world of dragon oil machines

and brown cattle. She needed the Andes to anchor her, bring her to life.
In the prairie lands there were no peaks, no mountains, no jagged, bright

wondrous rock to guide a lost pilgrim, an exile flung across the globe.
In the grassland there were only lost gales and souls, ones she had never

heard about. She had to make her own myths. My mother spent the first
decade trying to unlearn, trying to forget the heartbreak of the plane ride.

Act III.

My mother made her own myths, tried to unlearn the heartbreak of the plane ride.
That plane still haunts her now, forty years later. On the phone she asks, did we

do the right thing? Que piensas hija. Estás perdida? How to answer her, how
to say, yes, I am lost, but I am not lonely. Every week she watches the news

about children in the camps, feels the way that Spanish is still exiled from
her mouth. She wonders, perdí la cordillera, perdí mi país por esto?

I think about the idea of losing a country, isn't that what Bishop said, she
lost a continent once. But I know for my mother this is not metaphor.

It is her body suspended for decades in a language somewhere between
the wail of home and death lingering at night on the horizon. It is the sun

plunging into the widow lines of the dark. For my mother, what does it mean to lose a country, when English is now the blood language she dreams in

and the Andes are the shadows of other dreams. And here, in this massive land of ash, burnt bodies and brittle wings, she still cannot find herself on any map.

AUBADE FOR RICARDO

You look calm
like the ocean before the wind

catches it, shakes it awake, wide
with sound and aching. I have

not slept for hours, red eyed
in the darkness of the night.

My brain unable to grab sleep,
my thoughts like bullets

bursting out, erratic, staccato
speculations. I watch you

as the light breaks open through
the blinds, noting the movement

of your mouth, your eyes, your rib
cage, studying the heat of your

skin, the heat of your mouth as
you dream and sleep into

the next dream, the next
breath. I lie with you

my heart choking me, my will
shaken as I watch you sleep,

scared to wake you, scared
not to wake you, caught

knowing that one day I will
lose you, one day you will not

wake. And in that moment of
terror, when the light is just casting

its light on your face, I wish for one
thing only, that we face death together,

that both of us take the ride into
Hades hand in hand, in that boat

no one ever gets to leave, and we sing.

DEAR POEM,

You will not come. You refuse. You will not elucidate God or love,
the tendril vines and shapes of marriage, illness, the Oscar nominees.
You are silent, a cracked, yellow shell. I trust you for something,
anything. I want you to be curse and mantra. Instead you sit heavy.
You do not forget. You just do not reveal. An elephant in mud.
This is what emptiness must be. To spend the days stuck in front
of white spaces, imagining color. You demand worship and work.
You are a wicked queen with red lips and an apple, ready to kill.

1978

I
Like a brick wall, like a ruin from another time when
knights and dragons wandered the world in search of love.
The bricks are faded teeth that stick out of a mouth, jutting
out of the dirt landscape. A forehead with round arches
for eyebrows and missing eyes. The image is shot from below
and the furnace rises out like a wall missing a face. It is 1978.
There are people standing above it. There are people on the
ground below it. There are bodies inside the mine, though
no one can see them.

II
I am wearing a white t-shirt, maybe a blouse. My hair brown,
thick like steel wool. The picture blurry like something left too long
in the heat. Snow White is luminous, perfect teeth and a red plum
smile. Her hair a black, plastic helmet stuck on the top of her white
powdered face. There is yellow on her polyester dress. She does not
wear a crown. The sleeves of her dress sparkle, silver ribbon
wrapped around each puff, black and red velvet muffin sleeves.
I think now about how hot she must have been every day bending
down to hug children, freezing a smile for a 110-film camera.

III
The hornos of Lonquén are five miles from the Isla de Maipo. The Church
heard whispers about dangling socks inside a mine. A limestone mine with
a hidden, deep, dry mouth. A clandestine cemetery is what the newspapers
called it. If you look directly at the photo, you see a young man with straight
dark hair, a Beatles cut as my aunt would say. He is sitting on rock formations.
He seems to tower over the rest. He sits like he is waiting for the socks inside
the mine to grow feet and come out. Everyone is still. If you look at the picture
for hours, it won't change anything. You would not know really what

you were looking at. You would not know that everyone is there to see,
to know, to find the truth, some truth about the bodies inside.

IV

As a girl, I do not think I ever thought about the wicked queen or the old
witch or the apple. I did not think about the poison, that this girl was fleeing
from a mother and the envy for her lips and skin and teeth and hair. It is strange
to think about the story now, that the girl had to run from another woman,
a mother desperate enough to wish for her death. The girl ran into a forest,
into a strange house and fell asleep on a bed she knew nothing about.
She woke up to seven men looking down at her. Underground men, it turns out,
who worked in the mines all day purging the black dirt and rocks for diamonds
and other fairy things. How did the story of this girl not strike fear in
my five-year-old self? It does now, to think of the girl and her loneliness.
I coveted her red lips, red like a heart filled with blood, red like a secret
in the middle of the night. 1978, a princess and my baby-fat face.

V

In the picture of the mine, everything is so quiet, so still. In the quiet
fifteen men were taken from the village five miles away. Vans pulled up
to small wooden houses. Mothers answered doors. Sisters answered doors.
Wives and daughters answered doors, and the men were grabbed.
No old woman came offering an apple. There was no forest for the kidnapped
men to flee into, just vans and hoods. No one knew the story they were in.
In the picture, there is only the moment of waiting. Waiting for someone,
some underground men to pull out bones or teeth, or someone's gray jacket
or skull. When Luis Navarro took the picture, the people standing were looking
for the bodies, wondered about the bodies, wanted to find the bodies. No queen
had to hide her fantasies about killing or make herself into a leathered crone.
There was only a general and his machine for burying bodies. If you do not
know the picture, if you look at its grainy black and white pixels, you might

imagine it is still possible to find more than bones. You might imagine
the whispers were rumors, that the orders could not exist for such mines.
You could try. Many did try. There is no magic. Death always ends up being real.

Flying, a List

Halfway through a flight, I look around and think, *these are the people I might die with.*

Thousands of children have been thrown into planes, across the sky. No one knows where they have landed, if they landed, somewhere.

When walking down the tunnel to the plane, I am whispering rosaries to Mary and God. I say them under my breath like a song with no tune.

In small groups dressed all the same, with a guardian who demands the children speak to no one, they sit mute in the air.

When I was seven, we left a thin land quietly, never imagining we would not return. That plane ride is like my bones or breath, I dream it nightly still, even awake.

The threshold between the tunnel to the plane and the plane is holy, I cross over it as I cross myself.

There is a small sliver of joy when I fly over land and not water. My sister is afraid of sharks in the water, so now I also worry about being eaten in the water. Because I survive the crash.

On top of everything they keep hidden inside their skin, all the fear, the hunger, the danger, the memories of Abuelos and primos, they are hurtled across sky in metal tin cans to other states where no one loves them.

Cancer has done nothing for my fear of flying. I worry my whole self into madness just the same at 35,000 feet.

Children's bodies suspended in space, never having been on a plane. Ears popping, pressed against seats, metal buckles strapped across thin shirts. Safety instructions mumbled in hard English, hard like the desert, like barbed wire. The first journey.

ODE TO KODY

I have loved you for this decade,
   watched your wings folded into
      your chest, how the burnt brown
      hues, the white brightness of your feathers
flicker against the dirty glass cage
    heart and claws recoiled.
         Steller's sea eagles are far from home in south
western Pennsylvania. When I worked
    at the aviary, I would walk past your
      window, lean into the sunlight
speckled onto your body. You never
    looked at me or anyone, clung
      to branches of trees
      facing north. Your body rejected
    an audience of gawking kids, pink
skinned adults, trainers who loved
    you with frozen mice
      and other eyeless meats.
You faced no one. Never looked
    for anyone. I imagined you
      exhausted, lonely, even with a mate.
I imagined you wanted to stretch
    out the fifteen-foot width
      of your wings, catch air, light and sky,
grab the heat of the sun, glide along drafts
    looking for fish, not something mashed
      or frozen, with no life to gut out.
When you escaped, I cackled like I was
    the one who fled, like I was the one
      who found a hole in the wire mesh

like I was the one who wanted
　　　to fly beyond the rivers. I willed you
　　　to remember to hunt and break
bones with your beak. I followed
　　　your routes, your sightings
　　　　as you flew from everyone who
wanted to bring you back to an empty
　　　casket. I wished you enough memory
　　　　to leave that ashen place and find the ocean.
　　　Now that you are netted, returned
　　　　to a plastic world without blood
I still wish you other ways
　　　of flying.

STAGE TWO

You are invasive, like water through stone cracking gray
shimmers inside, like jellyfish in the Pacific swimming,
stuck to legs and arms, stinging skin in the sour brine.
Dark murmuration, wall of bones and feathers and small
bodies swooping through the sky, blotting out light and time.
Embryo soft mollusk tissue, thin membrane of life digging
for more life. How do you end up becoming part of me?
How did you find just the right cells and fat to live in,
to fuse with? It was you I felt that day, driving to work,
wondering about the thickness underneath my right arm pit,
feeling the taut skin raised above the nipple. You ate up
my entire breast like a hungry god, like the Cyclops craves
heads and men. Yet I always think of you as frail, as fragile,
like a sliver of moon before the sky swallows it whole.
A universe in five centimeters, seething for more.

El Rio Bravo del Norte

I do not know your bendings and rocks,
the architecture of your browns, wet grays, greens.
I do not know the curvature of your spine,
the twist of your body across the miles.
I do not know what lives you bring forth,
the javelinas, jackrabbits, green jays,
horned lizards you keep alive and feed.
Until a few years ago, I did not know
there were bridges to cross you, that you
were used and dammed up, that you
were a place of refuge, a place of light,
a way to escape from nightmares.
To be honest, until last year, I had not
looked at a map to see your edges,
your heart, the way you move through land,
where you supposedly ended and began.
I have lived far from your ways.

There are children in your dark waters.
They want to swim on rubber tubes.
They want to find fish, play with toys,
get their dusty feet wet, then run back
onto the shore, to fathers, to mothers, to life.
They want to swim like green-blue mermaids,
with black and purple hair. Keepers of water
treasures. Sirens of good luck.

You are the boundary, baptism of fear and hope.
I want the thing that divides us to be purified with you.
Maybe this is just my wish, my empty wish for

the dead to stop rising up from your banks and borders.
So many small hands and feet keep trying to swim
across, trying to reach the other side, the side of yeses,
the side of maybes and what ifs. Now, you are
a water grave. Some of us on one shore,
some on the other. Some of us still in the water.

FOLLOW-UP

And the risks, I asked, of a pill
that cuts out the hunger lurking

cemented to inside walls of my
stomach, the one you seem

invested in shrinking, in medicating
small, emptying like riverbeds in desert

heat. You said it was better to live
with ravaging cravings, covetous pangs

instead of feeding this body, my organs
whole. You were wearing all white

boots with a stripe of red along
the seams when you said fat

is a killer, think about that. Heart
attacks are dangerous to you right

now. These pills, they are safe
in case you want more than

fat. Obesity is the word you
actually used that Friday when

I forced myself into your office
wishing I'd taken off my boots

when the nurse weighed me,
hoping half a pound less would

show you I am more than
a patient who needs to

learn to starve herself.

OF NAMES AND NUMBERS

Frieda was Molly when we got her.
Who knows what she was before that.
Left behind when a man claimed the other two
but not her, gangly, thin, dark like pond water,
black holes, and soot. We picked her out
from the rows of cages lining the hallway.
She had no sounds, only breath. She said nothing.
She was silence and eyes. We brought her home,
half starved, swampy eyed, her coat matted,
dull from illicit days outside. She endured
the car ride pressed small into the corner
of the Subaru, resigned. We called her Frieda
thinking of the Frida of skeleton dreams, industrial
bleeding, and paint. But Frieda had no visible scars,
no bright, oil-based sadness. She had only a number,
faded blue inside her right ear, a tattoo before
she was Molly or Frieda, a tattoo before she was.
We never learned the numbers. They did not matter.
On her last day, we called her Frieda, like we did
on her first. On her last day, she knew her name.

What
  should
    I
   do with
      the left
        overs:
          left
           over love,
             left
              over
               grief,
               left
                 over
                  sorrow?
                    What
                      should
                        I
                        do
                         with
                          the
                          left
                         over
                         past,
                      the one
                      that gets
                      stuck in
                   the back
                 of my
                throat,
               the one
              that gets

hooked

into my

heart

my lungs

the one

that slinks

into the middle

of today, unnoticed

at first, yet growing,

half formed

strange

a Phoenix

charred in the fire

unable to grow

back wings

take flight

beyond

the sun.

These leftovers

never grow. Half

done things, aching

insect bodies with

out legs,

without

wings

without

mercy.

I have tried

so long

to sew on new

buttons, to plant

the unsprouted
bits. It is
like making
bread with card
board and crazy
glue. I have tried
to make space
for how they do
not fit inside any
boxes, how they
ooze out of every
thing like jellyfish.
Nothing works. The left
overs hide in the corner
like kudzu, crawling
up the walls, eating
up all the other
plants, choking all
the birds, coiling
themselves around
the furniture. Invasive,
unrelenting, they grow,
crustacean creatures, all
claws and eyes. Noxious
to all things, all new memories,
all new love. There are too many
of them to start over, too many
of them to hide. And I am left
with a raw heart covetous
for new seeds.

WHEN WE LOST OUR KINGDOM

When the wasps took over Oddfellows Hall
we hardly put up a fight. We hardly noted
the battle. We kept walking down the hallways
in states of despair, writhing in fits. At first,
we hid in our words or offices or maybe
the bathroom stalls. We looked at each other
like dying fish, mouths opening, closing, eyes
swelling out of our faces, our skin thin like wet paper.
When the wasps took over Oddfellows, we hardly
said any words. We hardly made any sounds.
We tried not to think about the wasps. We closed
the doors to the classrooms. Let them make
kingdoms on desks, inside the electronics cabinets.
We let them dance on computer screens.
We surrendered the chalkboards. We let them
fuck on the chairs. We let them bully us.
We let them drive us into the hallways.
We sagged. We waited for a queen.
But do wasps even have queens? When the wasps
took over Oddfellows they sucked out our swooning
sorrowful hearts and danced with all
their wings and eyes into the purple night.

At the Museum during Chemo, an ekphrasis

The Penance of Eleanor, Duchess of Gloucester
by Edwin Austin Abbey, 1900

She does not look like a witch
dressed in white, barefoot, wildness
still inside. To her left men, legs, arms
everywhere, like tentacles of an octopus,
glowing metal and chaos. Is there shame
in her body when she faces her husband
as if to ask for his share of her sorrow?
They are sealed in the middle of her penance.
He looks the sorcerer in black and purple clothes,
his bald head, lips slanted, seething.
As she gazes at the fullness of his body,
the sparkling jewels, the purple cowl,
her silence speaks a loneliness of burnt stars.
They say she called to unsanctified things
for favors better left underground.
They say she called the Witch of Eye for joys
not of the world of men. But what did she call
up when she begged for a child but love?
Frozen to her grief, hanging in the middle
of men and their clanging, their trials,
their declarations, their emptiness of hearts,
she had to walk for three days on stones
in bare feet. There is no blood, no red scars
but her husband's lips. She is suspended in light,
floating above the tangled bodies who try
to grab her gown, who clamor, crash
about looking for signs of her sin.

ALL LOVE STORIES ARE DEATH STORIES

—For Ricardo

The world is on fire. You tell me stories of love.
Your words dispel the shadows. They offer up the light.
When my mouth is full of nails, when I lie in the dark

you sing to my cracking insides, my blue blue heart, shove
away my pulsing sorrows, erase their lasting, biting blight.
The world is on fire. You tell me stories of love

of Odysseus, his years of wild suffering, of bitter luck, of
how he stabbed the Cyclops' eye, tricked him out of sight.
When my mouth is full of nails, when I lie in the dark

you whisper a tale of wandering, of lost love, of Zeus above
terrorizing men with gales, with monsters and his lightning might.
The world is on fire. You tell me stories of love,

whisper how Penelope weaved her shroud, hid her self - a dove
who secretly prayed for her beloved in the darkness of the night.
When my mouth is full of nails, when I lie in the dark

you feed me words and honey, keep away the wicked flood,
my madness, my demons, my sorrows bursting into flight.
Because, when the world is on fire, you tell me stories of love
even when my mouth is full of nails, even when I am in the dark.

I Continue My Love Affair

When I drive down 79, I don't usually pay attention to the sky,
the way clouds bend into the blue and green light. The car engine
murmurs. The steering wheel collects sweat. I propel forward
by habit, the years of moving down this highway every Monday.
I pack the car. I drink coffee. I move with the curves of the highway.
Big rigs swerve, muddle the lanes and I'm alone, suspended from all
time in the eighty-six miles between home and work. How weightless
the distance feels. Then, in a vivid turn, they appear, gray or brown,
white feathers luminous, sparkling of blood, rain, the dangers of living
near cement. One by one they show up, perched on light poles,
on highway signs, on stripped trees empty of leaves. Fierce, heads
turning, yellow eyes piercing, they watch the road, the metal cars,
the trucks. Sit in wait. Sentries waiting for time, ready to leap into
the air, ready to stoop into a field, grab a rabbit, gopher, groundhog,
pierce their insides, the soft middles, grip the bodies with talons,
snap necks, carry dead food to the woods, rip into flesh, and feed.
I drive by the drama too quickly, looking up, looking out the windows
of the car, wanting to follow them across the grass, into trees and bushes,
wishing I could leave the car on the side of the road, be an acolyte to their terror.
I am suddenly alive. I gasp in pleasure, crane my neck to see them fly
wild with turbine wings, black beaks, bodies that catch sky, slice through it.
I never know if they're hawks or kites or falcons. They are creatures of heat.
They are still somewhere beyond the highway and trees, living on blood
and entrails, restless for the next flight. Then I am a creature driven by blood,
by heat, ready to puncture the sky, grab bodies, find the innards, and feast.

I Dream of Abuela during the Pandemic

How does she know that I wander
around wishing a future, trying
to keep at bay invisible creatures
with thorns and death? Corona es
el pasado, she tells me. She laughs,
imaginate que antes la corona era religión.
Es verdad. I think the name is strange too,
corona, crown, and I have yet
to deal with crowns. My former
demons were those wild cells, but
they were spiculated, grew just
inside me, not wrathful
to those I love. Las velas son
el futuro, son el misterio del amor.
Mijita, prende las velitas ya,
Así se protege el amor.
I pray to her for strength,
for courage. I beg her, Abuela,
por favor, por favor, I plead,
deme su bendición. She laughs.
Ay mijita, lo uninco que te puedo
dar el la luz de las velas. And with
that, she's gone, vanished
like the sun drowning in
the ocean. I am left alone
with candles. I light them,
imagine a future with fire.

WRITING PROMPT

We think poetry offers a spike of joy,
like a bird of prey that dives across
the sky fierce with longing for the mouse,
the rabbit in the bushes, the bones
its beak will crack. That bird is
waiting for its kill, waiting for
the tendons in the gopher to
split, to burst forth with gorging
life, feed the hawk its fill and
stay quiet for the meal. That
might be what death looks like
every morning for the hawk,
for the rabbit, the groundhog.
That might be all that death
ever looks like. But you've asked
me to pick a noun that will help
me write a story that is not about
death, that even in its most opaque
colors might be worth the line.
I cannot. I cannot pick a word
that captures much of anything.
Except death. I can pick that word.
And here's this small token about
the way a hawk's talons crush its
prey, paralyzing the small creature
so it goes limp in the air, still aware
of the height and the blue it travels
across. Here's the word that animates
me every morning and every night
and every day of these weeks of
quarantine. What I can say is

I envy every animal already on
its death flight, that has let go,
has surrendered to the fatal bird hook.

Mixed Tapes

I was fourteen.

Madonna's "La Isla Bonita" sang out
our portable tape-deck,

the one my parents bought to listen
to cassettes family sent back and forth across

the mail. We listened with

the volume low. Whispers in Spanish
so no one heard our language of longing.

By then it was cheaper to call long distance.
Still those packages traveled 7000 miles,

carried magic and sorrow in thick
envelopes. I remember my sister pushing

play, listening to a language she could not
speak, then yelling into the machine

Hello!   Hello!   Hello!

begging my mother to tell her why tías y tíos, primos,
Abuela and Tata were not responding to her voice.

When Madonna sang "True Blue" my whole body
surged. We had lived in dual worlds so long.

At fourteen I had

no memory

of speaking to my father in Spanish. First immigrated
my parents wanted to mask all accents.

I learned later

how my father's students mocked him during lectures,
how my mother feared the grocery store because she could
not follow the cashier's questions. It's not often

but sometimes   I still hear the laughter

of my best friend in fifth grade. In her family's truck stopping
for gas, I asked if the truck took unleeded gas. Her whole
family cackled. I shook in the back, red

                              barely   breathing.

                                        I   carried

her mocking all the way through into high school, became
the mocker, laughing when my mother's beaches became bitches.

How my mother let me laugh at her
now seems the greatest act of love. She kept
quiet, let me think

I could leave

                              her behind.

A Burning

Four technicians.
Thirty doses.
Ten minutes.
Six weeks.

A world of burning
on a slab. Naked
from the waist up.

Scars. Sweat.
I forget I am not meat.

CV of Failures

—For Ricardo

My blue wedding dress slung over a closet bar, still
unwashed twenty years later.

Old student papers, stacked on the corner desk you pulled
off the curb on a Sunday trash night in grad school.

A pile of unread books on the nightstand, ecosystem
of neglect. I move them around every six months, thinking
it is about the order of the pile, not my life.

I could go on.

The size 10 red velvet pants I keep in the back
of the closet, imagining even now, two decades later,
my thick middle, stump legs will fit into them someday.

There's the file cabinet drawer with long-hand,
faded ink poems.

No way to blow life
back into them. They just sit,
fester, like insects

after a storm.

I could walk to the bursting garage in the back bulging
with neglected drills, rusted nails, earless stuffed animals.

I could tell you about so many half-lived projects and poems,
books, murmurings, flutterings, ambling pieces, the decades
this body bag of mine has dragged around on this world of earth.

I could tell you about them all, but I don't.

You have lived along
side my blood failures and star
promises, for years.

You know the thick gristle of this mid-life angst,
my sagging sack of bones. My whole, silly, empty bits.

And you. You dance around in the kitchen, beer in hand, avoiding
my piles of life unlived, missed moments, forgotten promises.

You say, come, come with me. Come with me. You take my hand,
force me off the couch, out of the house and my miseries.
We stand on the porch after the rain. It is brutal and humid and hot.
See, you say, it's not that buggy.

You hold me in the heat, sweat drips down my face.
Bugs suck on my blood, and I hold on.

EDUCATION

We were newly forming scholars.
Each class made us dizzy with vibrating fear.
Althusser, Foucault, Gramsci, saints of Monday
night seminars. I remember trying to find
your eyes, sitting across from you at the seminar
table so I could grab hungry looks at your hands.
Transfixed, I imagined the taste of your skin, your sweat.
I was in love with everyone. I was in love with no one.
The black-haired girl whose skin was velvet like porcelain.
In poems I called her Snow White. The guy with no hair
and small hands, who hated everything and everyone
but always came to the bar, drank dark, thick egg-soup
beer, murmured about love. I hated him too
even as I wished for his mouth on my stomach,
my breasts. How much of the first year did I spend
restless, longing for nights spent in wet pleasure?

This is a lie.

At twenty-three I never had
        such fantasies.
Never thought about
        grabbing legs, hands, pulling them, taking them into me
                        craving everyone
                                    because I could.

    Those wishes came later, after terrors

                                    like cancer
                                    choked me

breathless.

Cancer made even lust feel
     like work. I wonder now what coveting a body
         tastes like, what it is to want fingers and tongues
     to trace out the aching wonders

     still inside.

HORSES

A poem about those times when I rode a horse &
didn't know there would be those other times when
horses would make me feel scared to ride [because I
would not, might not stay on & I might eat more than dirt.]

$$\cong OR =$$

Horses $\cong$ the terror I have about the way they seem
like metal & meat merged together, ready to surge
across a field, use those thick, wide legs to dig up
dirt & grass, leave behind the echo of their hooves.

Act I scene I

In Oklahoma Lauren had horses on her farm. We rode them
bareback, no saddles, no reins, just the heat of their
curved back, my hands digging into coarse manes.

scene II

Never thought this might be dangerous. Lauren's mother
flung us over, hit the back of the horses & we took
off down the field killing flowers along the way.

scene III

Lauren called her family Mormon. I had no idea what that meant
except when we went to the grocery store, her mother scanned
ingredients looking for illicit sugar & caffeine. Stimulants, she said
matter-of-factly. Can't let the devil in the blood, she would smile.

≅ alternative to scene III

It's possible I thought this meant I was American = to ride
a horse (palomino, Lauren called it) across land that seemed free.

≅ second alternative to scene III

Those horses never made me panic = I rode like I belonged
to the farm & was a regular girl with a regular life, like I was girl
who had a name like Lauren & horses & a mother who believed
the devil could be beaten back by avoiding chocolate.

Palomino horse < Me + horses now

Horses + me since Lauren's farm = shady dealings = the time in
the Canadian Rockies & horse got spooked by black bear
> fear of riding after school with Lauren.

Epilogue

Oklahoma + horse + riding after school with Lauren ≅ me ≅ holding on.

Cancer is

chimera cells
seething for fat tissue
dry tongue thick
as a starfish sitting
in the sun too long
red sludge swimming
through veins
drowning
my green world

The Myths We Live

a loose pecha kucha after Fernando de Szyszlo

INKARRI
(Atahualpa/Atawallpa)

The red moment will come. That time
of future blood, when you, your head,
grown underground in the pit of dirt where
they kept your head away from the others,
the people who loved you, it will bloom.
You will burst into the sky.
Your body, severed for now, a map
of what is yet to come.

BÚSQUEDA

As a girl, I lived in the water, a fish
of sorts, with no fear of metal or hooks.
I did not live with sadness. I tasted the salt
on my lips, the brine of the ocean was
a gift. It tasted wild, like the world
at the beginning, right after the particles became
life. The ocean my world. Only later did
the sadness find me, when I left the water
for dry dirt and snow.

MAR DE LURIN

The Inca loved their children by taking
them to the snowy mountains, feeding
them coca leaves and beer, letting them
find the other side in the cold. I wonder
about their dreams, what they saw

as they waited to find ancestors
in the sky while condors flew around
them. Or maybe they had water
dreams, like mine when I left
a dark story, a country
stuck in blood and nightmares.

LA NOCHE

My niece suffers in the dark. Even at
thirteen she sleeps with all the lights
on, wrestles with nightmares.
I watch over her sometimes, remember
that dusk still haunts me, still forms
silent yearnings about things I cannot
see. We sometimes forget that in
the middle of the night, in the mouth
of the wolf, in the deepest ocean water
where creatures swim blind, there is still
a bright hope of living.

MESA RITUAL

I grew up Catholic. The closest
godly woman I knew was Mary
who, seemed to me, always accepted
the pain of her life in silence, or that
is how the story goes, the one I heard
over and over from old priests. Still,
her altars always loomed in my mind,
the dusk sky on the water, red

red like memory, red like a pulsing
open heart. In these tales of female
suffering, joy came as silence
as acceptance. I like to think of the terror
still inside her, the power of Pachamama
who is still out there waiting, looming
ready to rise out of any altar
burst out and strike.

UNTITLED

Atawallpa and his brother Huáscar
fought a civil war. They could not
know their own violence left room
for a crack, for Pizarro and his men
and steel and rage for gold. In the myth,
the Inca warrior comes back from
underneath the earth, puts his body
back together, restores his people
to love of Pachamama. How will he
put himself back together? His body
is severed, head and hands and legs
and arms buried far from each other.
In other accounts, the Spanish wanted
to burn him at the stake, put him in the pyre,
baptize by fire. Atawallpa converted.
Pizarro used the garrote. Even after the misery
of his head twisted off his body, the Spaniards
burned his skin. The warrior is still waiting
for the afterlife.

SOL NEGRO

There are myths I tell myself, when I
cannot imagine what morning will be
or how the light will emerge out of the
bright darkness of the night. I wonder
about the beginning of things, the mist of
first impulses, when the light opens up the sky
and the world is illuminated. I remember
the shadow parts of the heart, the blood
at the center, how once the ocean burst
out of that beginning, carried even the sun.

CAMINO A MENDIETA

My niece still holds my hand
when we cross the street or when
we walk down the street or when
we are at the mall, small and even,
sticky from chocolate or soda or
whatever she's been eating. She is
not ashamed to put her skin near
mine and sit with me in the heat.
Sometimes she tells me about her
nightmares, the bats or creatures
without eyes that reach for her,
fur and tentacles and metal bodies,
things like Cyclopes and other men.
She thinks about stars, the expansive
liquid dark, the stars that are already

dead and then, she cannot sleep.
That is when the eyeless things grab
her, so she lies very still and tries
to remember the sun.

PAISAJE

Now when I stare at the ocean
I look for the past, imagine the dark
water still has magic to give. When I
left my childhood ocean, the cold
bright blue world of joy, of pulsing life,
that place of all my people in one place,
it lived in my body like a spell against
forgetting. I still remember my loud laughter,
my blooming skin, the way the sun lit me
like a torch, like coral flowering from beneath.
It did not last, this blooming memory.
We left a war between men and armies
who did not know how to love (each other).
No ocean came with me. Everywhere
was a sea of white snow and ice.
I did not see the Pacific for a decade.

SOL NEGRO

There was a time when the Inca were
more than just bending heads
and wishing for the end. When
they lived in the sun like birds after
rain. There was a time when they

carried more than the salt in their own
hearts and looked to the sky, and they
knew the water, the taste of joy,
even in the darkness.

PARACAS LA NOCHE

Decades later it is impossible
to remember, to calculate all
the ways my girlhood was a dream.

LOS VISITANTES DE LA NOCHE

When I was a girl, I was also scared
of the dark. Not like my niece who avoids
the dark even inside. I feared the nether
worlds of the outside at night, when bugs
and stray possums and bats flitted through
a graying sky, when the sun fell slowly, dying
into the horizon and I was alone with
whatever happened after. When I was very
young, there were many things to note
in the dark, when men and tanks and guns
and other secrets grew in shadows,
did things to bodies like Pizarro did. But
I did not know this suffering. I only knew
the Pacific and its breath. My fear came later
when I no longer lived near the water
when the wind outside the bedroom window
grew monsters right on the glass and it seemed
they were just just just right there, and only

thin glass kept them out. They were ready
to grab my heart and devour it.

REGRESO A MENDIETA CARBÓN

· A few years ago, beneath mounds of
darkness and ice, archaeologists found
three bodies in the mountains, three children
mummified in ice, everything preserved,
even their eyelashes and small mouths.
They were curled up, legs crossed, pushed
into their chests and their faces slightly
melted, but the skin still there. They were
there for the ancestors, children chosen
to bring joy and beauty. It is hard
to look at them. The exhibit
curators put them in dark glass cases,
so that only if observers chose, they could
turn on the lights. But they belong to the ice,
to their people. They belong to howling
mountain and the gods who want them back.

CIUDAD VIVA

There is a sliver of orange burst
right in the center of the ocean,
like a star before it dies, like the sparks
of life right after the universe split
open and brought with it cells and heat
and other primal things. I wonder about

the astral bodies that got made in
that moment and movement
of swimming objects and light.
It must have been just blindness
at first, no distinctions of bodies
or rocks or particles, just the organs
of who we would become.
Our own myths.

PARACAS

I never think of Peru as a water
place. The Andes seem to be the
specter rooted in my mind.
Altitude and rocks and the edges
of mountain towns and stories.
But Pizarro had to land somewhere
with his men and guns and germs
and gray war heart. Many many years
before the Inca there were those with
a love of water, who buried their dead
facing the bay, bundled them in textile,
glowing reds, yellows, oranges, blues.
Like Atawallpa, their heads did not always
stay with them. Sometimes those left behind
still needed that life force.

VIENTO ROJO

The Pacific of my childhood
had a sticky, thick heart that beat

at the very center, like a drum.
The waves beat against the sand
quivering, vibrating reds, blues,
black, pulsing back and forth
like breath.

YANA SUNGA

In the land of no water
we moved to when I left
the ocean of my childhood,
yellow-orange grass grew like
arms and other body parts in
the middle of flat flat prairies.
At the time I thought only
half-formed, dark, tall creatures
grew there. As far as I could
see, there was only the wind
and the dry grass wailing.

RUNA MACII

At the center of every story is a red
sliver, the marrow, all the mashed
up birds and insects, all the wishes
and all the stars and all the breath.
In the center, the shadows eat the things
that have yet to crawl out, that have yet
to become. They live there in the pulpy
wound, like wild things waiting, waiting to
be released, to burst out. When I think

about the living things inside
the ocean, the tentacles and gills,
the fins and scales, the way they
pulse like a gasp, I think about
the frozen dead children, how their
stories are hidden between the dirt
and the water, how we think we know
only their silences.

DE LA SERIE TRASHUMANTES

Migration is blue. A heartbeat, the sound
of waves in a storm. Atawallpa did not want
to cross over to death. He was not ready to migrate
to the ancestors. But Pizarro skimmed
across the ocean, carrying some kind of god
and death in the belly of his ships.
He moved across the blue, like a whirlwind,
like a gale of gray disease. When he stood
on the shore, Spanish flag in hand, men gawking
from behind the cannons ready to burst.
All the wings of birds fluttering, flying,
wilding, swirling in the sky made
the whole world a tempest. Pizarro
the vessel of the nightmare.

EL INNOMBRABLE

I look at my niece now, all thirteen years
of her. She is a bird bursting, with voice
and wings, growing long and wild. She is

still unsure of the next migration. She is still
waiting for the sounds of unsung songs
to show her how to breathe, how to fly,
how to bend her body and become air.

CHEMOTHERAPY

Take my heart, smell its musky thickness.
Put it in your mouth, savor the tendons
the hard, fat veins, the alkaline red
blood. Let it sit on your tongue, expectant
tangy, like the mash of sea creatures after
a storm, mollusks, starfish, small crabs
all slathered along the sand and shore
dying in the heat of the sun
that   that   that   is

what you have left me with.

An aching organ, dripping with the stench of seaweed

hollow skin of meat and arteries

wounded

sutured with string.

AGNOSTIC AT 47

At church I sit alone, not ready
for the faith, luscious around me.

Small building with
the smell of stale incense
and dark wood. Windows
the color of wishes.
Surrounded by saints and stories,
my anger about God.

I end up there on Sundays
to feel the way solitude feels.
I wrestle God.

Sing   Stand   Kneel

The whole story
hunts me.
Birth, life, fall,
death   life again.

My mother arranges her entire body
around church, anchors
hands   mouth   heart.
She is certain, she knows his voice,
a rising phoenix.

In winter I force myself.
The wind cuts into my bones.
Snow muddles the drive.
I sit in the middle of that space.
No answer, still. Or I have only
this tender, wild answer.
I am waiting for the possibility.

Movie Memories

A faded polaroid with colors melting
a blotch here, a spark of light there.

Flashes, a short reel. I wear an orange
terrycloth dress with white stripes,

stand at the door of the hospital room.
My mother holds my sister in her arms.

A party for me, the next day maybe.
The terrace in back of the rented house filled

with dancing people, tíos, primos. I think
my Abuela is there. The beginning

of summer, the glow, the Andes are
sentries of snow and rock hanging in the sky.

My cousin is still alive, maybe
he brought his Dalmatian to the party.

Or a different reel. I'm at his house,
it's his birthday party the month before.

Are these two moments from the same
year of memory? I live with both playing inside

my mind like looping ribbons that float
in the wind. Other flashes, the house

in El Quisco. I found out years later a quisco
is a plant. In my earliest glimmers I smell

the musk of wood floors, the tart smoke
of fish cooking in the kitchen. My tío

at the door holding a fish the size of my body.
These are my dreams now, mostly.

I've gone back to Chile, to El Quisco
many times. Smelled the same ocean,

walked the same wood floors, stared up
at the Andes, the sky, the velvet sun over

the water, burning the sand. It's nothing
like the reels of my childhood, the ones

I pull into my body like breath, the ones I
seem to call into being when I least expect

them. They are not even in any language
I know or speak. Or maybe they are

when I see my other self, the fat little girl
who smiles and laughs and believes

love tastes like sugar, the salt and brine
of the ocean. That girl lived those memories

for decades in silence, no way to keep
the sounds of that time still inside

her heart and mouth. The most I can find
now is the joy of writing what feels

like someone else's childhood. Digging
for words, filling them with life, calling

the memories mine.

My Blue Blue Heart

If only I had legs like the taut
part of a drum, thin, curved, made
of muscle and sex and love.
I wish my body were not soft
like dough or pink and white
like the inside of guts.
Chemo days were like the inside
of the storm, a gray-green sky
erupting with bloody water.
I had jellyfish veins, a salty tongue.
My skin tender, ripe and sticky
like wet paste. Blinding needles
shooting through every organ,
liver, hips, hands, lungs. I was not
much then. Spent days thirsty,
craving cold ice wanting
to find a way to eat through
the pain. In the end, I found a way
to scoop out something like joy,
even that February when nothing
felt like my own and the snow outside
covered over every ray of sun.

How Grendel Tells the Story

There are men worth eating, and I've had my fill every night.
When the moon lights the way and I slink into the hall,
the hall they all love so much, with wood and carpets and men
all lined up ready for my feast. What do they know of my
shadow life beyond them in the cave of sorrow? They think I
stalk them because of hatred, cruelty. Do they not know the
need to feel warm, to find breath in blood and the tenderness
of skin? I was left for so long, so long, so long hidden from the
rays of the sun, the heat of the meadows in spring. I know they
think I am a tormentor, soulless and strange and eager for blood.
What do they know of suffering, the loneliness of loneliness,
when the only other creature who could love you is the mother
who keeps you locked away from the light of day? I'm looking
for the perfect body, the perfect skin, the richest tasting blood
to feed me back into the human I long to be, the son this king
denied when he saw my scales and teeth and hooves.

When We Still Believed

We fought about everything.
We fought about nothing.
We grew into stalking, strange
thinking writers, scholars, teachers.
We thought there was a heart in
the middle of every text and we swayed
back and forth between the struggle
and ecstasy of digging for the blood
of words, the guts of sentences,
the way a book could make our whole
hearts strangle our whole throats.
Ideas leapt out into our eyes, our mouths,
ripe, dripping, like the meat of a mango,
the way it smells of musk, the entrails
bursting from inside the skin. Those
were years of rushing, writhing, when
our chests gulped up all the green
the world could make and we
ran through the streets of Boston
like a pack of hungry wolves, ready
for the hunt, ready for the pieces of
a future we had yet to imagine. I
think about those years of surging,
when we felt our bodies stirring,
our summer years, when we were
still wild, when we still believed.

In Pennsylvania

Sometimes there is more love in a book
than in the whole day. As the darkness

bursts open, the pages offer words
lighted, bright despite the rain outside.

Ember moment of reading when
the hazy swirling possibilities are still

just beyond reach, and there's a pounding
ache to find the center of the story, the middle

soft parts, ripe and tender, the heart of fruit
just picked off a tree, the smell of wet dirt

lingering on the skin, my mouth anticipating
the wetness on my tongue. I've walked

the fields all day, sweating, cutting weeds,
digging out slugs, watering my paper crops

with vowels, with sounds, with song. I am
no farmer, no grower of food. I have always

hated the mud and dirt, smell of animal
shit. Still, I cultivate books as if all the fields

of my life were still waiting for new seeds.
What strange things can I find in a book?

That seems a small question. Maybe the
question should be, how can I live long

enough to eat all the fruit I've yet to plant?

Ghosts Don't Live by Our Rules

They aren't waiting for our love.

I have seen only the shadows of ghosts
though my mother swears she swears
she has seen her father's for years.

After church, when she goes into the kitchen for morning coffee, when she
gets into her car to take my nephew to golf practice, she says, si, ahí esta
esperandome.

Ghosts are the other side of things, son del otro lado, the world made of
shimmer promises and if we are as lucky as Mary Magdalen after Jesus
ascended from his cave, we will see ghosts, maybe even Jesus. Te lo prometo.
Jesús es parte del Espiritu Santo she explains matter-of-factly as if it's
obvious to everyone that ghosts and Jesus are in cahoots.

I do not know much about ghosts, about how they haunt or live or eat or
walk around. The closest I ever got to any ghost was one night at church
after the candles had blown out and it was time to shut off the lights in the
sacristy. I saw blue light walk across the center aisle. Maybe.

I would never tell my mother about the shadow.

She believes I'm an atheist.
I want her to keep thinking I don't believe in the body or the blood.
Ghosts on the other hand. Maybe.

Not Jesus who my mother's convinced is

     the first ghost,
     the ghost that guides all the other lonely sad ghosts up the stairs or

the sky to a heaven where ghosts have a place to lie down and sleep with dogs and maybe some stars.

This is what she says about the Holy Ghost, that he is Jesús and not Jesús. God and not God.

That ghost
has a lot of rules
about blood,
what we should
learn from
proverbs.

Like the one where ten bridesmaids waited for a bridegroom who was late, but it wasn't the groom who got in trouble.

Or the one about the landlord who paid the men who worked all day and an hour the same amount.

Or the one about the son who worked his father's lands, did all the tilling, never complained. Then his brother came home years later, broke because he squandered his inheritance, and the father rejoiced and killed a calf and gave him new clothes and shoes. The older brother got nothing.

It's supposed to be a story about how that dingdong was brought back from the dead and we should all be happy.

Or something.

Ghost Jesús-Jesus's main deal seems all don't-do's, don't-feels and don't-get-to's.

I'm not into ghosts who make you feel bad about trying to hustle some joy.

Still, there could be
something
else
some
other
shadows.

Like in the mornings when
the light through the curtains
and the sounds of life are muffled
      like everything is swimming in water,
      that half
      wide-eyed
      time
      when things are
      still being
      made
      in our hearts   there

                        could be ghosts
                        then.

                        Ghosts who are not God.
                        Ghosts who are like wildness.
                        Ghosts who are like love.

HEPATOLOGY APPOINTMENT

You tell me about the way fat lingers inside cells.
Fat cells will never go away you say. They fester

inside like bombs. Eat and they are triggered. Well,
that is not exactly what you say. You say once you

grow fat cells, once you have made them, they are
never killed, never lost even if you burn the fat,

the weight. The excess skin still hangs like a wet rag
around your stomach and behind your back. Well, no

you do not say that either, but it is what I wonder about
when you say fat can kill you. You know fat is something

to worry about right now you say. You are in danger
of your heart bursting on you you say. You are in danger.

That is always what you say. I have been having this
conversation for every waking moment of my life even

when I didn't speak English and my Abuela gave me
manjar, extra butter with extra bread at lunch while

my father yelled at her to stop feeding me so much love.
She would stare with those silent eyes, toast more

hallullas on the stove, carve out a pat of butter, spread it
on the bread, the heat making it a pool of sweet liquid.

You are not my Abuela in your angular glasses,
in your certainty. No. It's possible you must be

hungry all the time in that body you might starve.
Yes, you have the degrees, all the science of cells.

You have the hardness of small bones. You are
made for the chill of white coats and sterile sounds.

You are a gray stone. But have you ever known
the way love lives in the warmth of bread

on a fall day after school when your Abuela waits
for you, toasts all the bread she baked that day.

Lets you use all the butter.

When Ester Came to America

—after Richard Blanco

The flowers look obscene in their blood fuchsias and oranges
sprouting straight up between the round, thick bushes like alien
heads. The sun is above the frame and the whole sky glows
with raging summer blue. It looks thrown on with thick globs
of angry paint, but I think that must be the fading of color
in the print. She sits centered, like a queen, a statue dressed
in coffee brown linens. She must have been at least sixty but
Ester colored her coal-black hair black until she could not remember
the shade. The pineapple fountain towers over her, an indecent
bulbous, bulging shape. She is wearing the necklace I now own,
spoon-shaped copper pendant with llamas and the Andes etched in.
I do not remember much of that trip but the heat, the dripping
way sweat marked us all as we wandered in 98 degrees and humidity
that knocked Ester right out of her white and gold slip-on shoes.
My parents wanted to show her America, at least the parts in
the South near us. We went to Charleston that summer, stayed
outside the city in a rundown La Quinta Inn that smelled like
stale air and salt, drove into the city center with its brimming
oceans of tourists. This is one of the oldest cities in the South,
my mother informed her as we walked along the water toward
the market, trying to show Ester that yes, yes, yes, we are American
now. We are happy and free and satisfied with English. Ester melted
every day that week. We spent a week wet with the heat, drinking water,
wishing for ice, looking at "history." We never once talked about the other
South or other markets at the center of the cobblestoned streets, how they
used to sell more than ugly hats, barbeque rub, grass-woven baskets.

Before an MRI, a Questionnaire

1. Have you had prior surgery or an operation (e.g., arthroscopy, endoscopy, etc.) of any kind?
No ☐ Yes ☐

If yes, please indicate the date and type of surgery below:

> Once, I plucked the wings off a ladybug. I thought it loved me, so I pulled out the rice paper films. They oozed liquid. There was no blood. I was eight. I spent many months as a murderer surgeon.

2. Have you had a previous Diagnostic Imaging study or examination (MRI, CT, Ultrasound, X-ray, etc.)? No ☐ Yes ☐

If yes, please indicate the date, facility name and address, phone number, and body parts.

> The first time my breasts lit from the inside, I was forty-two. Cells grew. Spiculated morningstars swinging inside fat tissue. It was winter. I wore a large red sweater. My hair was long, coarse like horse hair.

3. Have you experienced any problems related to a previous MRI examination or MRI procedure?
No ☐ Yes ☐

> After the contrast dye moves through and up my left arm, there will be bruises, small spots of purple and gray veins. The technician asks, "how you doin'?" as the tube bursts with electric sounds, and I'm listening to Miles Davis's trumpet break through the noise. I think about the blooming, warm liquid slithering through blood. Does it look blue inside the body? "Drink a lot of water today," he says.

4. Have you had an injury to the eye involving a metallic object or fragment (e.g., metallic silver shavings, foreign body, etc.)? No ☐ Yes ☐

If yes, please describe:

> Small goblin jellyfish lymph nodes. They also had rogue cells. They gathered at my arm pit, lit up with the contrast dye.

5. Have you ever been injured by a metallic object or foreign body (e.g., BB bullet, shrapnel, etc.)? No ☐ Yes ☐

> My father was with me. He was lean with big, long, black werewolf hair and beard. I sat on the back of the bike and I tried. I really tried. He kept yelling, "keep your legs wide!" I think that's what he said. I do not remember the sounds from his mouth. I remember the spokes of the wheel bit through brand new school shoes. There was no skin on my right ankle. I could see right through to the bone, the web of tendons. I thought somewhere inside would be the answer. My father never stopped yelling.

6. Have you ever worked as a hobbyist or through employment in a metal shop, tool and die shop, or handled power tools involved in cutting or welding metal, or engaged in similar activities using metal? No ☐ Yes ☐

> I dream of chainsaws sometimes. They are my arms and I am metal blades and skin. In the dream, I cut through bricks, tree trunks, walls. Make windows out of silence.

7. Are you currently or have you recently taken any medication or drug? No ☐ Yes ☐

I was driving through the Appalachian Mountains. There were goats and other creatures bouncing around the green wilderness near the highway. Diagnosis = Obesity. Morbidly obese = BMI > 40. Obese. Obese. The doctor said, "take these pills." Take them and try for hunger. I was driving when my throat started closing up. A tingle on my face, hives bursting out from freckles. I drove, gasping. Forty miles to the hospital.

8. Are you allergic to any medication? No ❏ Yes ❏

Morbid obesity = BMI > 40. Am I still this equation twenty years later?

9. Have you ever had an allergic reaction to iodine, or any other contrast material or dye used for an MRI or CT examination? No ❏ Yes ❏

Don't forget to drink lots of water is what the technician always says after he helps me out of the tube, half-naked with no bra or shoes, no glasses so the world is swirled blobs of things, chairs, gowns, the metal door, the white-tiled floor. My mouth and tongue are dry.

10. Do you have anemia or any disease(s) of the blood, a history of renal (kidney) disease or seizure? No ❏ Yes ❏

What does the contrast dye do to organs?

2016-2020 = 12 MRIs, CT scans, PET scans $\cong$ how many moments of history I cannot get back? How many cells I cannot claim?

For female patients:

11. Are you pregnant? No ❏ Yes ❏

When my niece was born, she was an angry angry baby. Five pounds and something. Lungs like a crazed parrot, she spent her first three months flushed, red with rage. Her body would seize up tight from the cries out of her small fish mouth and she would become an immovable thing, arms raised, legs pulsing back and forth, her whole face blotted with blood. She seethed. I think she was not fully cooked. I think she knew about this raw deal of life beyond her mother's womb.

12. When was your last menstrual cycle?

My oncologist said "medically induced menopause. The goal is to shrivel your ovaries." Desiccated. Like dried up grapes. I hate raisins. They taste of sun after it's stopped loving bodies, skin. An enraged sun and then poof, grooved skin sucked empty.

THE JESUS I COULD KNOW

This is the night of darkness, the waiting
for Jesus to come from the depth of our sins
to return and find confused disciplines,
unbelieving of his wounds and blood.

I am like Peter, promising never
to deny him only to realize I care
about my skin. It is so much to
be asked to believe in ghosts,

bodies rising from the dead, to think
yes, carry that cross, take that spit across
your face, take those thorns and know
that this is love. I don't blame Peter.

Jesus was kind of a jerk, telling Peter
he would reject him three times
before the cock crowed. What's good
about speaking the truth

of Peter's misery, making him feel like
a traitor, a failure for not wishing to be
hung on a cross too? Isn't Peter the rock?
What this whole church is built on?

So, I'm thinking Jesus knew he'd turn out
to be faithful, a true believer. I mean, aren't
there thousands of epistles from Peter
to whoever? That one about love and patience

and kindness. This Jesus is off. As if you
need someone to tell you how much you are not
going to rise to your best self. Who needs
help figuring that out? But the other Jesus,

the one who begs his father not to murder him,
that man who is barely old enough to know
what love could be, who has to walk around
proving his whole life to others because his

father told some ancient prophets something
about salvation. That Jesus who wants to hang
with friends, drink too much wine, kiss a lover.
That Jesus who is so pissed off about poverty

he throws everyone at the church doors down
the steps for hawking their wares. That Jesus.
I get his lack of faith. He's like Thomas who
had to put his fingers in Jesus's side

to believe. That Jesus, maybe I'll sing to him
on Sunday mornings, wait for him on
Holy Saturday. That Jesus is like the bird wishing
to break out of the shell, that Jesus I could know.

When We Won Blue Jays at the Aviary

We walked around like silly, soft birds that evening,
dressed in peacock purples and bright blues as if
the world were made of light and champagne
and we could suck the whole thing whole, like an
oyster or an egg. All yolk and mucus, like the jellyfish
on the beach. That summer after chemo, I wanted
to find birds. We bought tickets to the aviary auction
and spent the evening talking to the birds, the huge
Kingfisher, lonely sad-billed bird with no one in his cage
to look at, the large Steller's sea eagles, angry at the wiring
above their cages, all beaks and claws, perched like statues,
eyes askew, slanted in disdain as we stared into the glass,
the small African Penguins strutting along the fake rocks,
bodies bobbing like buoys. You held the brochure
of items for auction. I tried to find all the birds of prey.
The food was terrible. Catered out of some place that
wanted all fruit to taste like paper. We drank stale wine,
walked around the rows of tables and stalls with art for sale.
I do not even like blue jays. They are loud birds with
banal colors and rude caws that sound like strange
car alarms. It did not matter. I had seen the blues
and oranges, the blue birds, the circle of white flowers
that still seemed to be dripping wet paint off the canvas.
The artist tried to explain her methods, how she chose
the brushes, the colors after months of studying the bird
collections stored at the Carnegie Museum of Natural History.
There are thousands of species all hidden beyond the displays,
she said. She spent months sketching bird claws, bird legs,
bird bodies. It's like a secret world of color she gushed.
You were polite. Asked questions about her techniques,

the choice of birds, why the whole painting seemed off-center. She told you about the preservation processes for the birds. The feeling of sheer surprise at each new set of birds she got to touch, draw, paint. We placed our bid for the blue jay painting. The rest of the night, I thought about the dead birds in the drawers of the museum, hundreds of bodies, lying flat in paper, lifeless and limp, draped inside drawers, stillborn.

My Hands

My hands no longer carry things easily. They still
tremble when I try to braid your horsehair in summer,
when I grate a lemon for soup, when I work them
around your crown of locks. My hands are like
the hands not made of hands anymore. They are
leftovers. I've bitten the nails to bleeding stubs
of mashed meat. But you still ask for my dough
hands to pull out the snares of hair, to wrestle
with curls and smooth out the bouncing red
wire ringlets. I take the time before the world
swallows you in its light, before you leave the harbor
of the house and jump into the wideness of the ocean,
before you no longer want to sit still in the summer
afternoon letting me work out the roughness,
the stray curls of your kingdom. For now, you sit
with legs swinging, eating a mango, sucking the fruit,
a hungry succubus and you say, tell me a story
as we wait for the heat of foam curlers to spark.

THE MIRAGE

I go to church not
because I think God
is there. That deity has
a funny way of being absent.
All mirage, like a bird's song
in a tree, no body, no feathers,
just a burst of sound from
somewhere in the gullet.
That is God and I'm not
looking for a hero.

At church the whole building
radiates voice. Sometimes I think
all the saints on the windows
will melt off and slither away
from that low murmur of
aching whispers, the cascade
of unfinished longing that
throbs out of our mouths.

That waterlogged feeling,
that knowledge that there
is nothing to imagine about
God beyond quiet emptiness.
I go to church for that bright
misery, free of any phantoms
that God is more than
the voices in a small room,
writhing in hope.

Here is where the tumor grew, a small hill with wild ants, browns and blacks
the size of grains of sand, or maybe the size of gray water-worn pebbles.

It grew here in this yellow and brown second-floor room, where students come
trudging up the stairs in the bleak light of winter, sit and cry in my purple chair

about mothers, exams, insurance bills. In this room, where I hand out Kleenex,
it grew, like kudzu along the walls, lace of green, thick veins and tendrils, like

the curl of a question mark. When did it start to bloom, this tissue, this mound
of fat and cells with teeth? When did it burst through the walls, thick like rope,

a tight, hard rock vibrating heat? I grew here too, young scholar, bright from
the nightmares of graduate school, arrived already blue after battles with

theory. In this room, I started reading again, for the first time it seemed.
Gathered up books, blood, wanted to remember the joy of the thing. How

much I longed to find more than flaws in metaphors after graduate school.
In this room I tried for magic. I tried to be more than being lost. I tried for

something like love. Now two decades in, what am I exactly? Not as new.
Not as tender. Not as. But words seem small for this metamorphosis. As I

learned again to feel what time can do for the scars of learning, this tumor
grew. A silent bomb, a shadow coal creature without light. These cells found

life inside me, made whole universes with mitosis, clung to the soft parts of
my body and flung themselves into living like wild fire in a parched forest.

After all the months of poison, of mouth sores and night terrors and sweat, I am back in this room again. There is an aching, silent hole inside my right breast.

The room is still the color of canaries after rain, the books, the words seem never to have left, as if they burrowed a place inside the shelves, a home of black ink and

paper. Again, I sit here in this room of my life, after the war with raging cells, waiting to find the world new again, waiting to see what this body and love and time can do.

Notes

"Bonebreakers": This poem was inspired by the Valley of Dry Bones story from Ezekiel 37:1. In this story God gives Ezekiel a vision of bones coming to life, a prophecy about the future life of the nation of Israel. When I was drafting this poem, children from the Americas were fleeing homelands, crossing deserts, rivers, oceans to escape structural violence; by structural violence, I mean violence that is inherently integrated into structures that are imagined to be neutral but are ideological, as is, for example, the structural violence of immigration systems.

"Gravity, or after the Plane Crashes": I was inspired by Samuel Taylor Coleridge's poem "Rime of the Ancient Mariner" (1798) when writing parts of this poem. The phrase "slimy creatures" is a phrase derived from it. The original line in Coleridge's poem is "slimy things did crawl with legs/Upon the slimy sea."

"Writing Poetry after Turning 46": This form is one that I conceived in a poetry writing workshop I took from GrubStreet Center for Creative Writing. I thought of the idea of moving through time and affect and imagined the waves of the poem mirroring these interwoven concepts.

"1978": This poem references a photo by Luis Navarro taken in 1978 of mines in Lonquén Chile where the remains of fifteen men were found. They had been tortured and murdered by Augusto Pinochet's junta as part of his strategy of killing and disappearing Chileans who were opposed to his dictatorship. In her book *The Insubordination of Photography: Documentary Practices Under Chile's Dictatorship*, Ángeles Donoso Macaya argues that images like Navarro's and those of other documentary photographers of the dictatorship era, especially the Lonquén photographs, were "used as denunciatory photography" and "not only brought to the fore the worst features of military repression—illegal abductions, clandestine killings, and forced disappearances—but also became visual documentary matter—physical traces, icons, and symbols—of a horrible and unrepresentable crime" (86).

"At the Museum during Chemo, an ekphrasis": This painting, "The Penance of Eleanor, Duchess of Gloucester" (1900) by Edwin Austin Abbey, is at the Carnegie Museum of Art in Pittsburgh. It's a painting I have gravitated toward for many years. Edwin Austin Abbey was an American painter, muralist, and illustrator whose work is featured in the Pennsylvania State House and at the Boston Public library. Given my own biography, I like to think of this piece as tied to my time both in Boston and Pittsburgh.

"I Continue My Love Affair": I think of this poem as a continuation of a poem in my book *I Was a Bell* called "Someday I Will Visit Hawk Mountain."

"Horses": In the summer of 2020, I had the privilege of taking an intensive workshop facilitated and taught by Porsha Olayiwola at GrubStreet Center for Creative Writing. The writers in this workshop were generous and brilliant; they and Porsha gave me incredible feedback. I drafted this poem in that workshop—called Risk, Restriction, Rebellion—using amazing prompts Porsha crafted. We had a week on a topic about pop culture called "Name Drop: Pop Culture as Timeless Relics." Several of the poems we read for the week used typographic symbols. I was inspired to try using them as well. I have tried to go back and look at notes to see which specific writers I might have been in conversation with and I've asked my former classmates too. Here are the pieces we read that I know helped me think about typographic symbols: Hanif Willis-Abdurraqib "4 Poems From The Crown Ain't Worth Much,"; Sotère Torregian "The Ghost of the City of New York Appears in California, May 25, 1971,"; José Olivarez "I Walk Into Every Room and Yell Where the Mexicans At,"; and I know there are others I'm forgetting. I am also grateful to my colleague Adrienne Krone for her counsel about Mormon Studies.

"The Myths We Live, a loose pecha kucha after Fernando de Szyszlo": This poem was developed from a prompt and series of images in Sara Rivera's poetry workshop as part of GrubStreet Center for Creative Writing. The pecha kucha is a presentation storytelling form in which speakers present twenty images or slides and have twenty seconds of commentary for each of the twenty images. Terrance Hayes developed the poetic form of the pecha kucha specifically in his poem "Arbor for Butch." Fernando de Szyszlo (1925-2017) was a Peruvian abstract artist who worked in multiple artistic forms. The title of each of the vignettes of this poem are titles of his paintings Sara Rivera presented to students as prompts for the pecha kucha. Several of the titles of the paintings I use in this poem center the stories of the Inca. In this poem I interlace the story of Atahualpa/Atawallpa and narratives of immigration and childhood.

"How Grendel Tells the Story": My husband and I read Seamus Heaney's *Beowulf: A New Translation, bilingual edition* aloud to each other across 2020 and 2021. This poem was inspired by this practice.

"Ghosts Don't Live by Our Rules": This poem borrows its title and first line from Viet Thanh Nguyen's short story collection *The Refugees*. The story "Black-Eyed Women," where this phrase appears, is about a mother and daughter who are visited by the ghost of their son/ brother. When they discuss these visitations, the mother tells her daughter that as a ghost, her son appears in his own time, or "ghosts don't live by our rules" and describes ghosts' relationships to love and the human world when her ghost son begins to visit. I've written about this story's influence on this poem when it was featured in *The Iron Horse Review*'s National Poetry Month issue in April 2023.

"Before an MRI, a Questionnaire": The questions in this poem are adapted from the standard questionnaire for Diagnostic Medical Imagining. Other medical diagnostic phrases in this poem—like MRI, CT, Ultrasound, X-ray—also appear on questionnaires and assume patients who fill out these forms know what they mean. These kinds of questions assume bodies are in need of being managed, often diagnosed as deviant from the "standard" healthy body, and in need of monitoring.

"Oddfellows 215": I think of this poem and "When We Lost Our Kingdom" as companion pieces about the role workspace takes up in my body and mind. This is my office in my academic building.

Many poems in this collection—including "Let Emptiness Be the Prize"; "Movie Memories"; "Horses"; "Cancer Is"; "When We Won Blue Jays at the Aviary"; "Ghosts Don't Live by Our Rules"; "Before an MRI, a Questionnaire"; and "Oddfellows 215" (and so many others!)— were written, revised, and given feedback across several workshops. These include my local Squirrel Hill Poetry Workshop, those facilitated and taught by Porsha Olayiwola and Sara Rivera at GrubStreet Center for Creative Writing and Allison Hedge Coke's workshop at Macondo. I also subscribed to Two Sylvia Press's National Poetry Month prompts in April 2020; many of my wrestling-with-God poems emerged from these prompts. I remain ever grateful to the poets who allowed me space to write and revise in their company and who offered generous feedback on drafts.

Gratitude

I would like to thank the journals, editors, and readers who continue to believe in my work. I am, as always, grateful for the support I receive from my poetry teacher and mentor, Rebecca Morgan Frank. I would also like to thank my local poetry communities, including the Pittsburgh Poetry Workshop writing group and my local bookstores, especially White Whale Books and City of Asylum for the incredible work they do. I would not be the writer I am without my family, my father, and especially mi mamá, Macarena; my sisters, Montserrat and Javiera, and Natalia, my KitKat ahijada extraordinaire, all of whom continue to be endless sources of joy and love in my life. I would also like to thank Aimee, co-conspirator and collaborator; Amor, we keep growing up together; Barbara, a bright sharp light in the gray; Missy, pun-lover and lover of all things Chile; and Stephanie, who is now on the side of knowing what hell cancer is and who fights it with all she's got. Finally, there are no words for what Richard means to me. He is my beloved. He is my home and my first reader.

BIOGRAPHICAL NOTE

M. Soledad Caballero, professor of English and Women's, Gender, and Sexuality Studies department at Allegheny College, is a Macondo and CantoMundo fellow. Her collection *I Was a Bell* (Red Hen Press, 2021) won the 2019 Benjamin Saltman Poetry Award. *I Was a Bell* was the 2022 International Association of Autoethnography and Narrative Inquiry book of the year and a 2022 International Latino Book Award winner. She is an avid TV watcher and a terrible birder.

www.ingramcontent.com/pod-product-compliance
Lightning Source LLC
Chambersburg PA
CBHW021508090426
42739CB00007B/522